The Golden Ratio Trading Algorithm

Discover the 9+1 Bulletproof Strategies that Helped 113 Dead Broke People Get Out of Debt

By

Golden Inner Circle

publisher for any reparation, damages, or monetary loss due to the information herein, either directly or indirectly.

Respective authors own all copyrights not held by the publisher.

The information herein is offered for informational purposes solely, and is universal as so. The presentation of the information is without contract or any type of guarantee assurance.

The trademarks that are used are without any consent, and the publication of the trademark is without permission or backing by the trademark owner. All trademarks and brands within this book are for clarifying purposes only and are the owned by the owners themselves, not affiliated with this document.

Author: The Golden Inner Circle

The Golden Inner Circle is an elitist group business incubator. It's a way to speed yourself up with far fewer setbacks. If you are already on track follow these enlighten entrepreneurs to take you to the next level of your potential.

Get the support you need to:

- free yourself from negative limiting beliefs

- develop a marketing strategy that works

- discover the Golden Method to improve your skills

- realize the dream of being able to work in complete autonomy

- create passive income with low-budget investments form your home.

The Golden Inner Circle is the movement that is leading hundreds of people to find a real strategy to achieve great results in the most profitable businesses such as Youtube, Instagram, Airbnb...

This series of over 20 books called "Clever Entrepreneurs in the XXI Century" is a step-by-step program that will take you from zero to the highest level of success.

The information contained within will help you to raise the dormant leader inside you, develop the King Midas' touch and to embody the NEW Golden YOU.

Table of content:

Introduction:

Defining your corporate plan lets you make the best of your opportunities so you can accomplish your objectives. A successful business plan may be the difference between living and flourishing.

Some companies grow to a stage where the entrepreneur can no longer manage it themselves. Now is a perfect opportunity to start dreaming about a plan that can lead the company to accomplish its goals, e.g. by encouraging people to make choices. Getting a well specified approach to achieve your company goals will also help you clarify your plan to your staff, networks, sponsors, consultants, borrowers, accountants and investors. It's vital for moves like finding finance.

Overall, the effect of a successful plan is that you remain efficient over the long term, stop making typical errors, and stay ahead of the market. A plan provides a common understanding of your goal, making everybody in the company appreciate what you're working for. It will support you:

- Prioritise work

- Make the correct decisions

- Say 'no' to distractions

- Make the best of your place in the marketplace.

When you're experiencing loads of rivalry, developing a plan involves recognizing your benefit and your optimal place in the business. Then you should schedule things to reach you there. In this guide you can find lots of things to focus on so now it's up to you how well you select certain strategies and incorporate them in your business.

Working on a plan will help you discover your keys to progress, and set a course to follow towards reaching your goals. It may also help you grow into new goods or services. Without a consistent business plan, you might make choices that clash with each other, or end up in a bad financial and competitive role.

Chapter 1: Become a YouTuber

Until you even make a video that has viral value (making videos is not incredibly difficult if you enjoy what you do), you have to develop a platform that sticks out. It is also accurate that the videos you produce are the chemical X that will make your channel highlight. However, I have noticed that building a killer channel before releasing the first video is crucial. Let me also figure out that we shall not discuss how to build a channel; what we shall discuss is how to create your channel and make it stand out. Here are the ideas you need to accomplish this:

Create and design your brand

We will not cover, as I have indicated, how to create a channel. I should point out, however, that if you have a Google email and comment account or like YouTube videos, chances are, you already have a channel. It is important to note that your YouTube brand is at the heart of the channel you create. This is what's going to prompt viewers to sign up for your channel. What this means is that the proper attention it deserves must be given to your channel's name. The name of your channel should be memorable and relevant to the content you're going to share with your subscribers and the world. For example, you might create a channel under the name 'beauty within if you want to create how-to-make videos.

If you don't know how to build a channel, here is the link to the portal for creating a channel.

Exude professionalism

You will notice one outstanding thing, which is the quality of video and interactions if you take a second to wade through all the videos that attract many views and comments on YouTube. This simply implies that you have to be professional to create a killer channel and video that draws in millions of views. You need to be skilled in your presentation, how you make the video, and in particular, the technology you use to shoot the video. This means that you can use your iPhone (not recommended) if you do not have a video camera, but make sure to keep the phone as steady as possible. In addition, the audio on your video should be of excellent quality. It also suggests that you should seriously consider adding subtitles to your video if you are not a native English speaker or have an accent. I can guarantee that your channel will never come close to the status of stardom if your videos are out of focus. Visit some of the more popular channels to find out what is professional by YouTube standards and emulate their video presentation.

Create a video response

Despite the fact that they could generate high-quality sharable material, most YouTubers fail to get their channel noticed. This leaves the uploader with only the possibility that his or her channel may be found by anyone with a broad following. Here's a trick to make sure your channel is out there more easily. The trick is to produce a video answer to a famous video of high quality. In addition, to guarantee that other individuals click through to your platform without actually caring who you are, make your answers either informative or extremely divisive. Video answers that are divisive, fascinating, surprising, or informative can also guarantee you a few subscribers who believe your perspective or design appeals to them. On the other side, even though you don't receive viewers, the chances are good that a couple of your videos would be viewed by anyone who clicks through to your site. Using video responses is a caveat; make sure you do not attempt this trick until there are some really good quality, interesting videos on your channel.

Bait the crowd with reviews

The first thing you probably do anytime you want to purchase an object is to head over to Google to look for ratings. Video analysis is the quickest and more likely to go viral. As long as you make sure that the analysis is thorough and appeals specifically to the crowd of people involved in that specific thing, it really does not matter what gadget or item you review. All of us still search for product feedback (perhaps even you); as such, build a platform that gets many views and subscribers. The endeavor to create a few highly measurable review videos of some famous devices or items is well worth it.

Channel your energy on the channel

If only every three years your favourite musician produced a song, how would that make you feel? The word is Bored! A very similar approach is taken by a YouTube channel. If your commitment to the channel waivers, all the subscribers and subscribers you have gathered will drift off to another channel that consistently offers them videos if it takes you very long to upload. Uploading doesn't stop; you need to be active on the channel, interact with viewers, respond to their comments, and just make sure they feel appreciated and connected to you. If you do seem to keep your audience's interests at heart, they will move on by constantly interacting and uploading videos.

Key point/action step

To develop the mindset and routine necessary for creating an outstanding YouTube channel, fall into the habit of logging onto the site daily, watching a few videos and commenting on those that interest you. This is especially important because it will fuel your idea machinery and push you to create videos that people like.

How to Apply What You've Learned?

I am aware of the fact that too much information can work against you at times; the same applies to your journey for YouTube stardom. To help you out, I have decided that all we have learned will be summarized into an actionable plan that you can easily follow. Let it get to us.

Fuelling your idea tanks

Draw your ideas on YouTube from other videos that are doing well. I can guarantee you that there are other YouTubers in the field, regardless of which field or category you intend to upload to. Visit their channels, view their videos, and take away the best practices from their videos. Watch how they make their videos, voice-overs, etc., and then find out if you can replicate their style but add a flare of personality.

Viral does not come easy.

It is not easy, as stated earlier, to create viral videos. Sadly, to create viral videos, there is no trick or outright blueprint.

There is only one definite way, on the other hand, to ensure that your videos are near perfection and closer to viral, and that is practice. Practice using various cameras, different lighting, and even different angles to create videos. You increase your video creation abilities when you employ this tactic. Make sure you don't look back in simple terms and say, 'I should have shot that angle differently.'

SEO plays a very central role

We looked at the numerous variables leading to the YouTube and Google rankings. Optimizing the video and platform is key to this rating. This suggests that to make the video rank higher, you have to read what you can about keywords and how to use them efficiently. Fortunately, the internet is full of tools you can use for SEO and keywords. You don't even have to use paying keyword queries since Google's free keyword analytics service works best.

Engagements make all the difference.

Through commenting, enjoying, and uploading their footage, you must actively connect with other YouTubers to push traffic to your channel and posts. When you create video responses to widely famous videos, this is particularly successful. In addition, commitment ensures that you have to interact with YouTube regularly by making and sharing videos as much as possible.

Chapter 2: Create an Instagram channel

What is Instagram?

According to Wikipedia, Instagram is an online mobile video sharing, social networking, and mobile photo-sharing service that allows different users to take videos and photos and then share them on different social networking platforms like Flickr, Tumblr, Twitter, and Facebook. As you can see from the description, it is a mobile app for smartphones and is available on Windows mobile, iOS and Android.

With the app, you can add captions and filters to your photos, get likes, and increase followers tremendously. You can also follow friends or whoever else you like to get their pictures on your Instagram feed.

If you are awfully talented in taking amazing pictures or want to turn your many followers into customers, there are many ways you can begin to earn money on Instagram.

A brief history of Instagram

Instagram was officially launched around 2010 and three years later became one of the largest and most engaging social networks. It's no wonder why Mark Zuckerberg, the Facebook

CEO and founder, bought this photo-sharing app for a whopping amount of 1 billion dollars from its rightful founders (Mike Krieger and Kevin Systrom). Most people thought he was crazy. At the time of purchase, Instagram had only 13 employees had less than 22 million active users and no website. It has since grown so fast to currently have more than 300 million active users, definitely more than Twitter or Pinterest and over 100 employees. In fact, according to recent research, people are spending more time on Instagram than on Twitter or Facebook. It's the fastest growing social platform in the world, and its future is very bright. Just as it has upgraded Facebook's balance sheet, it can upgrade your income. Instagram's social feeds and easy-to-use editing tools make everyone capable of creating and sharing nice edited pictures today. It has empowered people in unexpected ways, even those who don't bare Bieber, Hilton or Kardashian names. You can use it to share your interests, for instance, skateboarding, art, and other experiences, or just share your photos or videos and make money for such a simple effort. Many big companies are now using this platform to reach out to customers worldwide, and their sales have skyrocketed. Companies like Puma are even hiring Instagrammers with massive, profound, and engaging followings at more than $5000 a day to capture photos that display the respective company products.

Key Point

With over 300 million Instagram users, anything is possible. Think of it as a large billboard in a large intersection where over 300 million people frequent, and you will discover that this is an immensely big number of people. So, whatever it is that you might want to do, whether to gain in popularity or to make money, the potential is limitless.

Basic Tips for Making Money on Instagram

Like many people out there are doing, you can turn this so-called hobby to be a money minting cash cow by following the basic guidelines given below;

Build a follower base

Getting people to follow you is the first step to making money with Instagram. Without a very minimum of a few thousand followers, it will be hard for you to convince any brands to sponsor your posts. Even with the over 300 million users, it doesn't mean that being on Instagram automatically qualifies you to have access to this large number of users; you must strive to get a fraction of this number to follow you. Just like any other product, before you start making sales, you need a market, and this is your followers. Here is how:

1) Increase followers; Take all the time you need to expand on the number of your account followers by interacting with your followers and posting unique photos. You will learn more about this in the next chapter of this book.

2) Use hashtags to attract more people. For every photo you take, make sure that it has at least three hashtags that can add to your viewers. The hashtags should speak about the photo but should be broad enough to show up in numerous searches. Don't worry! You will learn more about hashtags later in this book.

Upload quality images

1) Master your craft; the fact of the matter is that if your photos aren't so good, people will not be willing to buy them. This may mean many different things to different people, but you need to take quality pictures if you want to end up selling them.

2) Use different cameras; avoid limiting yourself to your phone's camera. With Instagram, you can upload photos taken using other devices; all you need is to transfer them to your phone first.

Get yourself a nice camera and notice the significant difference in the quality of photos you take.

Set Up Your Store

Without an online store, you are almost doomed. You can't sell your photos via Instagram directly, so you have to set up an alternative way that people can buy your pictures. Here are some ways you can go about this.

1) Hire a store service; you can sell your photos directly through Services like Twenty20 and soon through their site. You get 20% of the sale, and they handle the printing and shipping for you.

If you want to avoid dealing with printing and shipping orders, this can be useful.

2) Get your own store; you can use your personal website to set up your own online store. You will definitely get more money than you would if you used a hired service, although you will have to take care of orders, as well as shipping and printing the images. For each image you upload to sell on Instagram, it should have a caption containing a link to its store page regardless of which method you use to set up your storefront. So that the link doesn't take up the whole caption space, use Tiny URL or Bit.ly to shorten the address. Take advantage of apps such as 'Hash Bag,' which automatically identifies and posts any items that have the hashtag '#forsale' on your Instagram account to their respective market.

Market your Products

After you gain followers and therefore in a good position to approach and convince any company, do this:

1) Contact companies; you need to explain and convince your target companies how you can help increase awareness for their brand through your Instagram account. Show them how often you update your Instagram feed and give details on the number of followers you have. Carry some sample shots to display and illustrate you know how to take clear, artistic pictures which can shed some positiveness to their product. Services such as Popular Pays and QuickShouts can connect you with companies, which hire aspiring Instagram marketers.

2) Work out a contract. You need to have a clear written contract indicating matters such as the expected number of pictures you are supposed to take and bonuses for the improved number of followers, if any. To protect yourself from being underpaid by the company you are marketing for, sign a contract.

3) Take quality pictures of the service or product. For sure, you wouldn't like to upload a mediocre or bad photo of a product you are supposed to be marketing. For you to keep the contracts coming in the future, you need to play your role as an ambassador for a given product effectively and uphold the expected standards.

You are free to add some personal touches to the photo, and in fact, you should. You don't want your followers to feel as if this is just one of those advertisements they would spam so easily if they weren't following you. Your followers need to relate to your image on a personal level.

Turn your many followers into Customers

1) Point followers to your blog or site; you should have a link to your company's or personal website or blog always on your Instagram profile. As you continue to gain more random viewers or followers, traffic to your site will also increase. Emphasize your skills. You can showcase your abilities and

talents on Instagram, including fashion, web development, photography, and several other fields. Update your current projects and latest work on your Instagram feed always. Remember to use hashtags to attract potential buyers to your image.

2) Take your product's photos. If you run a business that deals with physical items like vehicles, cupcakes or whatever, one of the best ways to advertise your merchandise to new people are through Instagram. Take photos of some of your latest products, then make sure you use hashtags to entice more followers. Some hashtag examples include the product name and use, your company name or slogan. If you have a store page, make sure you link to the product's image comments. Remember to submit the nicest photos you got of the product and avoid those low-quality cameras at all costs.

Offer Brand Takeovers

You can earn some good money by doing an "Instagram takeover" as a substitute for sharing sponsored posts on your own account. It's exactly what it sounds like and is all about posting photos on another person's Instagram account. Either you can get temporary access to the person's or company's account, or you can be asked to supply photos, additional descriptions and hashtags to them. This works especially well for travel accounts, "We supply 5-7 amazing images to a company or tourism board and they feature our photos showcasing how we see the destination," says Bouskill, an Instagrammer.

Sell Your Account

You can sell your account for profit once you have a tremendously successful account. You can even get a six-digit for selling accounts that have 500,000 to a million followers.

Key point

Stay active on Instagram to get as many followers as you can, upload quality images of what you are selling, set up an online store, market your great skills to companies, and then turn your devoted followers to customers. Do "brand take over" or sell your account if you please. Don't forget to put the links and the hashtags on your Instagram images or comments. When you do that, you can watch your bank account swell in due time.

How to Post Memorable Content

You need to create posts that will stick in people's minds for a while. Here are some ways you can do this:

Take unique and interesting photos.

This may seem so obvious, but simply taking good pictures is one of the best ways to get followers on Instagram. Instagram is flooded with pictures of people's cats and meals, so have well-shot photos to set yourself apart. Let the pictures you take related to your audience fully. People are hesitant to follow you if you always post images they can't relate to. It doesn't have to be a "perfect" photo to be good. Good photos are more human, and any imperfections make them more so.

Put a boundary on "selfies." You can post some 'selfies' on Instagram, but don't let them dominate your account. Your followers don't want to see you but rather want to see your photos. You can seem narcissistic if you post constant selfies, and this can put off many followers. Sad as it may be, there is an exception to this if you are very attractive. Posting attractive pictures of your gorgeous self can drive many followers to your account. Still, don't let this take over your content!

Post Every Day

You need to have a new post every day and post reasonable several times if possible. Your presence must be felt all the time. With this, your follower's list will grow every day.

Add filters

Instagram became so popular because of the filter options. These filters fine-tune the colour of your photos and give them a more "real" feel. There is a variety of filters available on Instagram, so feel free to try out several until you identify the one that works well with your photo. Don't use the same filters too often, or your images will start to seem too similar. #nofilter is a popular hashtag on Instagram; if the picture is too striking to even need a filter, use it!

Place captions on every photo

You will be amazed at how fast you can turn an okay photo into a remarkable one with a good caption. Your viewers' attention is grabbed by using a caption. The more people you make smile or laugh using a caption, the more you'll retain them as followers. Cute captions or jokes are particularly trendy.

Utilize apps for extended editing control

While you can slightly edit images on Instagram, there are many apps for both Android and iOS that can provide a lot more tools. Use these apps to darken, brighten, crop, add effects, text, and so much more.

Popular editing apps are Afterlight, Photo Editor by Aviary, Bokehful and Overgram.

Create collages

A fabulous way to show a collection of images or progression is to make a collage to post on Instagram. You can do this using several apps, including InstaCollage, PicStitch and InstaPicFrame.

Post your photos at a good time

Since Instagram is an extremely popular service, your followers' feeds are probably constantly updated. Post your photos at the right time for them to be seen by as many people as possible. Make sure you post photos in the morning and after the end of normal work hours. Instagram photos normally stay around a person's feed for 4 hours so if you want your followers to actually see your images, avoid posting them in the middle of the night.

Most Beautiful Photos

Not only do you need to post consistently, but you also need to post beautiful images, which are instrumental to increasing your Instagram followers. You can even be featured in media houses for outstanding photos. You need to inspire people through your photos and not shock them out of your account.

Avoid Posting All Your Photos at Once

The necessity to post photos regularly does not mean you post all the photos you have taken at one go. If you want to post more than one photo a day, make sure they are spread out in the day. Share one photo every three to four hours. You don't want to make your followers oversaturated with images-keep them yearning for more. Don't just dump all of your photos at the risk of making your followers start passing over them.

Pick up an Insta-Style

Like most successful Instagrammers, you need to develop a signature style for your photos.

Whichever technique or filter you choose, make sure your photos stand out from the crowd.

Chapter 3: Make money through binary options

What are the options?

Options are financial securities that give the consumer the opportunity, but not the responsibility, on or before a certain date, to purchase or sell an underlying financial commodity at a certain amount. Just as you know, with specified terms and conditions, options are like every other financial asset or instrument. It is important to note that options are not assets themselves, but their values are derived from other financial assets such as stocks, hence the name derivatives.

Two styles of choices are primarily available; call and place. Call options grant you the opportunity to purchase an underlying one at a given price on or around a specific date in the future, but not the responsibility. Call investors are betting that the value of the commodity will grow in the future and thereby allow them the ability to make market profits.

On the other side, placing options gives the customer an opportunity, but not the duty, to sell an underlying commodity during a specified time at a specific amount. Placement buyers conclude that rates are expected to collapse in the immediate term.

Why options trading?

Options have been branded as some of the riskiest investment ventures. However, over the past decades, participants in the options market have tremendously grown. Why would an investment vehicle think to be so risky to gain such popularity? There are several benefits that are attributed to this, but let us shift focus on the two main reasons why people use options hedging and speculation.

1. Speculation

Speculation is better understood if thought of as betting on the price of an underlying asset. People base their beliefs on what the security price will be in the future as the market adjusts itself and make a bet on the predicted market movement. The use of options for speculation is what makes options a risky venture. You not only have to be accurate in determining the direction of the market movements but also the timing and size of such movements. Let's say you predict that the price of Microsoft stocks will likely rise in the next three months; you can buy the call option, which will enable you to buy the stocks at a lower price and sell them at a higher price. If the market moves in your favor, you can make substantial gains. However, if the market movements do not favor you, you lose 100% of your investments (options price).

2. Hedging

Options can be an insurance policy for your investments. You can use options to hedge your investments against a downturn. For example, if you assume you wish to take advantage of the upside of technology stocks like Microsoft, you can buy a put option and take advantage of the upside keeping the stocks safeguarded against any downturn.

Key point/action step

Investing is all about determining the kind of investor you are and the goals you hope to achieve in investing. When investing in options, you have two main reasons for investing; to either hedge or speculate. It is important that you determine your reason for investing in order to invest wisely.

Types of binary options

There are many types of binary options available to you as an investor. Interestingly, the most common types of binary options not only confuse new traders but also experienced ones. I will go slow just to ensure that you get this information clear.

1. Digital binary options

Under this, we have call/put and up/down options.

Call options: You place a call option if you believe that the price will rise above the entry price.

Put options: You use this if you believe that the price will not rise above the entry price.

With up/down options, you only need to predict the direction of the price movements when you entered the market. Will it move *up/down?*

2. Touch binary options

These types of binary options come with predefined rates needed to win the trade as opposed to the trading participant just predicting the direction of the price movement. Here, you predict a level of decrease or increase it will reach (touch) and the level it will not reach (no touch). Please note that these types of binary options only trade when the market is closed, mostly during weekends. If the market touches or passes the specific level by 1700GMT on Monday, you get your returns. No-touch pays when the level defined is not reached.

3. 60 seconds option

Are you the type that gets excited by quick rewards? Perhaps this is your best bet. This option expires in 60 seconds. With this, it is easy to predict price movements. Basically, I usually recommend this option for traders who wish to profit quickly from a trending market.

4. Boundary options

This is sometimes also called range options. It differs from digital options in that two-level supper, and lower are defined. The asset must stay inside this boundary for a trader to receive any payout. This method is ideal for stable markets when trading inside the boundaries and volatile markets when trading outside the defined boundaries.

Key point/action step

As you have seen in this chapter, there are different types of binary options that you can invest in; hence, it is important to choose wisely. My advice would be to start small with binary options that are easy, for instance, the boundary options that give you more leeway when it comes to anticipating price movements. However, it is up to you to choose the most suitable option to trade-in depending on the returns you are looking for. If you are the adrenaline junkie kind of investor, then the 60-second option is most suitable for you.

Chapter 4: Social media advertising

There are a great many ways to earn money through social media. What we'll discuss for this chapter are the more straightforward methods of making money from your social media accounts.

More than 50% of all internet users all over the world go online for social media. This goes without saying that websites like Facebook and Twitter are huge opportunities for advertising and marketing, and many have taken advantage of the situation by allowing people to earn by displaying advertisements on their profiles.

This is especially profitable for people who have large networks and can be considered 'influencers.' Influencers are those who have a great number of followers and therefore have more powerful recommendations.

Earning can work in several ways. Once you display a Facebook ad, you can earn when someone clicks on the link, makes a purchase and leaves their mobile number or email address.

One can also go for paid tweets such as SponsoredTweets.com. As the name suggests, you get paid when your followers click on promotional links via Twitter.

Pros: Displaying Facebook ads can give you around two cents per click, depending on your arrangement with the advertiser. Sponsored tweets can earn you $6 for one tweet for 2000 followers and can reach up to $1000 for those with a massive following. Given the amount of time that you actually spend on your social media accounts, the rate is fair enough.

A good thing about displaying ads is that you are totally in control of the content that you wish to display. This is also an opportunity to help your followers by making quality recommendations while earning at the same time.

Cons: What seems to work for social media ads can also work against it. Most people really don't like ads, and so coming up with advertising links that are catchy enough to warrant attention may be tricky. Too much hard selling can also turn off some of your followers. It may not be as effective for people who have not yet established a large network of followers.

Social media advertising can be a very lucrative venture; however, it also highly depends on the extent of your social network.

Chapter 5: Stock trading

If you find yourself with more saved cash and an appetite for risk, stock trading may be a good venture for you. To describe it simply, stock trading involves buying shares of certain companies for a particular price, then selling them afterward for a profit when the value of these companies rises.

While it does sound easy, comprehensive research must be done before one engages in stock trading as it's not uncommon for people to lose their hard-earned money when the economy stumbles, and the prices of companies suddenly crash. Smarter traders can get profits of as much as 600% in three years, but this is backed by long years of experience and the 'feel' of the stock market.

Here are a couple of tips to earn extra money from stock trading.

Be in it for the long haul. Patience has always been a virtue, and the same holds true for stock trading. You will need to learn to apply the "buy at the low and sell at the high" law, and it requires a lot of patience to keep yourself from buying just because everyone else is buying because chances are the price maybe a little too high, and it will affect your profits.

You also cannot expect a 30% profit right away in your first year of trading, as it may take five years for you to truly realize your profits.

Buy great companies. One of the things that make stock trading a hit is a fact that your earnings depend on how well your company performs. That being said, a great deal of research must be done on a company before you decide to buy a piece of it. Does it have a good management team? Does it have years of experience to show for its stability? How profitable is it? Many experienced investors say that you should only buy a company that you truly know about for you to understand how it will be affected by key events.

Diversify. Another good tip is to not keep your eggs in the same basket. Do not focus all your investment on a single company to keep yourself from crashing with it when unexpected events take place. It is always a good practice to invest in various industries to create a buffer for your investments.

Chapter 6: Blogging and freelance writing

Blogging

Blogging is one of the most common platforms for web content on the internet and can be done by almost anyone. It is a form of social networking that allows you to create your own comprehensive content where you can showcase whatever you wish.

Blogspot and WordPress are some of the leading blog posts where people can sign up for free, and it allows anyone to publish their content online. If you have a knack for writing, this one is for you. You can post a wide array of content, from blow by blow accounts of how your day went, reviews of the latest movie you watched, opinions about current events, social commentary, book reviews, advice for mothers, shared experiences about pets and many more. Writing can be done for self-expression or to share experiences that you believe can help other people.

As fun as it sounds, establishing a blog isn't a walk in the park because you will need time and commitment to update it with quality content to keep readers coming back. Junk content that is simply copied from other web pages will easily be disregarded as plagiarized content and will not help the reputation of your site. It is also recommended to find a niche topic that you can focus on so as to target a specific brand of readers and establish a regular following.

A golden rule for web content: quality is king. If your readers find that your website offers something that they cannot easily find with other webpages, they will keep coming back. More readers mean a better reputation for your blog and, therefore, higher potential earnings.

Earning through blogging can be done by leasing your webpage space to advertisers, by writing sponsored reviews or blog posts about particular companies, or by selling actual products.

When you gain a following, people keep coming back to your page. The more traffic you get, the more attractive your page becomes to advertisers because they would want to take advantage of your page views and use it for advertising their product.

Using this concept, various sites offer bloggers the ability to display advertising banners on their webpage and get paid for them. There are hundreds of sites that offer these services, and some of the most popular are Infolinks, SiteScout (formerly Adbrite), and Clicksor.

You can get paid from $0.01 to $2 per click, depending on the value of the banner. The more traffic you get, the higher chances of people clicking on the banner link, and therefore the more money you get.

Other companies pay for impressions, meaning visitors really don't need to click on the ad for you to earn; they simply have to 'see' it. This has much lower payout rates but is also more convenient to use. Bloggers strategize on the placement of their ads to come up with more clicks and more impressions.

Google AdSense is one of the leading providers of blog advertising. They are the most popular; they provide the highest payouts but are also the strictest. It is recommended that you purchase a top-level domain (www.ebook.com instead of www.ebook.blogspot.com) for them to approve your request. They also go for top-notch quality as all pages with traces of plagiarism or copied content are immediately disqualified. They also strictly screen the nature of content that they approve to ensure that it only provides quality information for potential readers. If one passes through the rigorous screening of AdSense and keeps working on improving their blog quality and traffic, they can expect earnings of $0.15 to $15 per click, with most getting up to $48 for 1000 visits, the highest among all advertisers.

For those who have established a reputation with their blog— if you are a mom known for providing valuable baby-care advice, a girl known for fabulous taste in clothing, or a guy popular among bloggers for keenly observing gadget updates—some companies may want to bank on your influence in the blogosphere by sending you free products to review or by asking you to create a write up about their brand for a fee.

This can be a tricky line to tread, however, as some readers may get 'turned-off' when they find that you are being paid by companies to make positive reviews. A good way to work around this is by providing 'full-disclosure' to your readers by telling them if a particular post was sponsored by a brand. You may also want to keep your tone from getting too patronizing to keep your blogger's integrity intact. This way, the trust system between you and your reader is maintained. Another great thing about blogging is that the manner in which you create your posts and how you build your reputation is entirely up to you. Therefore, anything that happens is really under your responsibility.

Another great way to monetize your blog is by selling products. You may have some handmade crafts that others may find useful or a friend who knows a great supplier of accessories and clothing. Instead of renting an actual physical store, you can just post your goodies on your blog, advertise them on your social networking sites and receive orders from people. Selling with this method normally involves having the products delivered to your customers, so make sure that you also know the procedure for shipment.

A lot of people have earned a living by selling online products and relying on social media and word of mouth for their advertising. It's a pretty hassle-free method because your online space is mostly free, and you invest in your product and seller reputation alone.

Blogging is a great way to earn money online, but it takes passion and commitment to keep it going because the internet is flooded by all types of bloggers, and sometimes it takes a special flair to stand out.

Blogging is not as easy as it seems, but if you've got what it takes, it can also be the most rewarding.

Freelance Writing

Freelance writing is another way to earn online through the power of the pen—or in this case, the keyboard. Several bloggers venture to freelance writing and vice versa, while a lot of them actually juggle being both. The key difference between blogging and freelance writing is that with the former, you are in full control of the layout and content, and you write for your readers on your terms. Freelance writing, on the other hand, is pretty much like outsourcing your talent for their purpose, and therefore all articles are written on the client's terms.

It may be easier or harder, depending on which side of the fence you're on. But freelance writing will definitely give you a more reliable stream of income once you've got the hang of it. Beginners can start on sites like Odesk.com or Elance.com, where potential clients and freelancers can meet to discuss terms and gain an interface for communication. The more experienced ones eventually gain contacts of their own and can get projects for higher rates.

Articles can range from a simple 400-word description of products or 30-word description of hotels to 4000-word essays or long sets of blog posts. Formatting and tone of writing can also vary, which will require flexibility and good writing skills. A strong command of grammar and spelling is a basic requirement, along with the ability to consistently meet deadlines. This also includes the patience required for hours and hours of research.

Freelance writing can be as demanding as a day job or even more. However, it still allows you to manage your own time and decide which projects to accept and which to set aside for a later time, as long as you meet the expectations of your client.

Beginners can earn about $30 to $50 an hour, while the more serious ones can earn as much as $80 for an hour and even $2000 for a month.

While these sound like really good money, one must be aware that the life of a freelance writer is anything but easy. Here are a few tips that one should bear in mind when aspiring to become a freelance writer.

Get ready for rejections. Because of the increasing level of competitiveness that this industry requires, one must be ready to experience multiple rejections of their articles. Remember that they are not rejecting you as a person, only your work. Only when you are able to resist taking rejections personally will you be able to hope to make a living out of freelance writing.

Keep your reputation clean. Your reputation as a freelancer can either make or break you. Being able to consistently submit deadlines, work according to your agreement with the client and provide quality work are sure-fire ways to boost your chances of being referred to new clients.

Socialize. Go out, meet people and socialize. This is another way to develop networks and attract potential clients. Learn to market yourself.

Set your goals. Are you content with making $1000 a month, or would you like to earn $2000 or more? Set your goals according to your family situation; if you find that you can get a lot of more than 8 hours a day for freelance writing and that you would like to earn a significantly larger amount, then you should go for higher-paying clients and better writing gigs.

Seek help. Hundreds of websites are available for freelance writers who would like to improve their craft or would like to get the hang of the technical matters involved in the trade. Take advantage of these groups in order to meet fellow writers and keep yourself motivated.

Chapter 7: E-book publishing

If you are a book lover or enthusiast, at one point in your life, you may have dreamed of publishing your own book and being a world-renowned author. You might have sniggered at the thought back then because getting published seemed too far-fetched and ambitious. What if you learned that you can now be a full-fledged author of your own book for real?

The landscape for book-reading had changed quickly since 2012 when e-books outsold hardbound covers for the first time. More and more people have been turning to e-books because of their easy accessibility and portability. In no time, self-published authors gained popularity as well. Digital publishers are making it unbelievably easy for people to publish their own books, and many are taking advantage of this opportunity. Several authors are finding themselves easily selling a thousand e-books a month and are definitely outselling their hardbound counterparts.

If you have an idea sitting in the dark corners of your mind for quite some time, now is the best time to write that e-book, and who knows, it might just give you your first million! Here's a rundown of how:

Write. There's an initial draft that is basically your brain spilled over pages of chaos, a review draft that finally organizes your thought and develops what you really want to say, and the polished editorial draft ready for publishing.

This is, of course, the most important part of the process because, without publish-worthy content, your book will not sell a dime. Focus your thoughts and define your goal straight up — would you like to entertain, inform or inspire?

Formatting. This involves making use of the digital publisher format for your e-book and coming up with a cover. The design of the cover is critical for people to take an interest in your eBook. Take note that it also must be attractive even as a thumbnail because that's how your eBook will initially be presented.

A lot of self-published authors try to design their own covers with awful results. It is recommended to hire a professional cover designer to create a more polished look for your book. If you're going to earn thousands of dollars from it, you might as well invest, right?

Publish and Promote. Head over to your digital publisher, login to your account and follow the pre-defined steps to publish your e-book. You must have your tax info ready for royalties and legality purposes.

Pricing is a very important aspect. Most e-books are priced at $2.99 to $9.99. However, it is found that most readers buy e-books in the $2.99 to $5.99 price range. Price it too high, and no one will buy it, but if you price it too low, you may not gain enough profit.

There are many digital publishers out there like Nook, iBook's, and Smashwords; however, they have already established themselves as one of the most credible sites for online transactions. The intensive feedback system is top of its class, and they help to extend the reach of your book even to people who have no idea who you are.

Promoting the book is critical to the success of your e-book because no one will buy it if they don't understand that it exists. Make extensive use of social media, offer incentives for every purchase, or advertise it in online forums and blogs. Take advantage of the digital nature of e-books to spread awareness. It may take a lot of work, but it's definitely worth it.

Publishing e-books is a great way to leave a legacy on your passion or expertise. Now is the best time to do it!

Chapter 8: Make your own video games

Your Debut into The World of Making Video Games

I am very tempted to tell you that the video game industry is a gold mine waiting for you to prospect, and indeed, it is. I am also tempted to tell you that video game creation is only a success story only for big game companies, but alas, I will not. Why? Because I would be telling you a lie. In the interconnected technology-driven world, which is where we live, anyone, and I mean anyone, can create a video game.

Do not get me wrong; I am not necessarily proclaiming video game creation success to all. I am merely stating the fact that thousands of people across the globe have been able to make their own games. Here is another fact; long gone are the days when video games had only two platforms: computers and gaming consoles. Today, with the advent of mobile technology, video gaming has gone mobile. With 98% of the world's population being owners of a mobile phone, it is only right that the video game industry would take advantage of this. Again, today, there are more mobile phone-based games than there are computers or gaming consoles in the world. What does this mean?

It means that the fruits are ready for the picking and that the pickings are in plenty. It means that if there ever were a time to get into video games production, now would be it. Contrary to popular belief and media hype, you do not need to be a geek with 'mad' coding or programming skills to create a video game (this does help, though). Anyone, even you, can create a video game. All that you require to create a game today is a bit of know-how, a lot of passion, and tons of patience. I am not promising that your video game will be an overnight sensation. I am also not promising that the journey will be easy. In fact, it may be very hard. What I promise you is that by the time we are through, you will be in a better position to create video games and well on your way to making some money from your video game creations.

Key point/action step

Although it is possible to make your own video games, you need creativity, passion, and patience if you are to become a success story.

After writing up your concept, hashing it out, and reflecting on it, it is time to fuel that enthusiasm train. Unless you are a serious video game creator with a few thousand dollars to fork out and some experience in pro programming, Unreal 4 Engine is not for you, albeit being one of the best video game creation engines. For the rest of us, who do not want to start from scratch, neither do some serious coding, we must rely on the help of software. Fortunately, the web is full of free and premium video game creation software. What I have found is that in a world of choice, most people are unsure of what to choose. It is important to point out that most of the software available each has different features, merits, and demerits. Your choice of software is entirely dependent on your game creation needs and level of expertise. I must also point out that you can do much using the available software that we will discuss shortly.

Before we move on to that, you are probably wondering why you should use an engine. Why not program the game by hand. I can give you a couple of reasons. However, I shall give you just one substantial reason. Engines provide a host of developmental tools, which aid and simplify the creation process. Furthermore, they are time efficient and less complex compared to hand programming. An engine also makes it easier to manipulate your AI (artificial intelligence), sound, and graphics.

Before I give you that list of software, I have to point out that some software is best suited for 2D graphics while others work best for 3D graphics. Above all, and regardless of your engine choice, most engines do come with tutorials to guide you in usage and creation. Here are the engines you can try to use.

Game maker: Platform-Windows and Mac OS X

The game maker engine is a product from YOYO games. It is a comprehensive engine well suited to help you create beautiful games without necessarily being a programming whiz kid. However, the program does require some getting used to (learning curve). Fortunately, the program does have a tutorial, manual, and a very vibrant user base and community ready and willing to provide you with answers to pressing questions. Unfortunately, only the light version, which does not allow for more robust features such as export, is free. For the premium version, you may have to pay up upwards of $500. Additionally, I have found the engine interface to be a bit lacking in terms of design. One of the more outstanding features of the software, both the free version and the premium version, is that you can port your game to different operating systems such as android, iOS, desktop, and HTML 5 (Web) with no basic knowledge of scripting or coding. This makes it an outstanding tool for a beginner.

Construct 2: Platform- Windows

If you liked Game Maker, then you will most definitely like Construct 2. Like Game Maker, construct 2 is also a premium engine that comes with its own user base, tutorials, manuals, and active community. Unlike Game Maker, construct 2 does not offer a free version. Instead, they offer a free 30-day trial of the full engine. Because the engine base is HTML 5, it is the best alternative to web animation tools such as Adobe Flash or Java. Using this engine, you can create beautiful 2D games that you can easily port to Windows, Linux, and Mac PCs, as well as Firefox Marketplace, Chrome Web Store, and the iOS and Android app stores. This means your games can be available on many different platforms. Unlike Game Maker, construct 2 has an appealing and robust user interface. Additionally, the engine has an in-built event system that allows you to instantly program actions and movements. The premium software costs about $120. However, if you want to use the commercial package of the engine, you will have to pay $400.

Stencyl: Platform- Linux/OS X/Windows

Stencyl is probably the most popular engine. More than 120,000 developers, with over 10,000 games published games across the globe used it. In its simple form, the engine does not require any programming skills. However, if you are tech-savvy, you can write code within the program to create more advanced features and functions. The engine has a drag-and-drop feature that adds to the easy use of the engine. Unlike all the other engines we have looked at thus far, Stencyl is not an all-out by. Instead, it works on a subscription basis; a $200 annual subscription basis; the $200 is for the most expensive (and comprehensive) package.

The engine offers cheaper discounts for students and game design experimenters. Because of the subscription nature of the engine, developers tout it as the easiest way to make some quick money (this means that the engine is commercially driven), rather than it being a fun way to experiment with video game designing. This does not mean that once you create your game, you have to submit it to them for sponsorship (which they offer)!

Flixel: Platform-Open source

Flixel is an open-source video game creation engine. This means that regardless of how you intend to use it (for commercial or personal purposes), it is completely free. This engine is very versatile. You can use it to create a wide range of 2D vector animations. The software itself runs on the backbone of ActionScript 3, an object-oriented programming language. ActionScript 3 adds a wide range of development tools to the program. These tools allow you to customize the engine. If you are looking to create filmstrip games or 'epic' 2D animation with side-scrollers, this is the 'it' engine. However, I have to point out that despite its versatility, Flixel cannot handle 3D modelling. On the other hand, I also have to point out that the tile-maps at your disposal in the engine are fulfilling and intuitive. Additionally, the engine has a plethora of camera functions; the in-built save game function and the pathfinding design all make this software one worth trying. Because the software is open–source, it has a bit of a C-style programming learning curve. I must point out that this should not stop you from using the engine. Why not? Because the open-source nature of the platform also means it has a wide user base and a thriving community.

Unity: Platform- OS X/Linux/Windows

If your aim is to make outstanding 3D video games on a budget, Unity is the choice for you. Unity is an outstanding fully-fledged design/development suite. The engine has a free version for personal use. However, for the commercial version, you must pay $1,500, i.e., if your aim is to create commercially viable games. Let not the money worry you, as the free version of the engine is something to behold too. The software, even the free version, can port to up to 10 different platforms, not limited to mobile and desktop. It is also capable of delivering crispy clear video and audio.

Key point/action step

Regardless of which engine/software you opt for, you will need to familiarize yourself with it fully if you really want to derive the most benefits. Therefore, I recommend you create your video game with a starter mentality. Additionally, if there are functions you are not sure of, turn to the online user community. They (community members) have a wealth of knowledge and are always willing to share

How to Publish and Market Your Indie Video Game

With more and more developers publishing games out to a hungry lot of gamers, generating downloads and sales for your games is harder than it has ever been. Do not despair; here are some tips to publish your game and get it noticed.

Publishing your game

Like any other store in the category of apps, your best chance for success in publishing your app is variety. Depending on the platform of your indie game, submit it to as many stores as you can find. This will ensure that more people get a chance to view or download it. Additionally, when publishing your video game, make sure that you fill out every single detail.

When you visit a store for submission, there is usually a game heading (what most of us call Meta tag), a game description, and an overview. Make sure to fill out all the fields. Also, make sure that you fill everything out correctly using keyword-rich sentences. What do I mean? If you are filling out the heading of your game, make sure it is something relevant to the scope of your game. If you are filling the description and overview field, view it as a marketing platform. It is your chance to tell users why they should download or purchase your game and what makes it different. Publishing your game is very standard and uncomplicated.

A key point you must note and a mistake that many developers make is that they fail to post their game in the right category within the store. If your game is a racing game, make sure you specify the category to increase your chances of discovery.

Marketing your game

Marketing your game is more difficult than it sounds. Moreover, it is the single most important thing to do if you are not creating video games for the fun of it. Therefore, you must create a marketing plan. A video game marketing plan is no different from any other product-marketing plan. You must set out well-defined goals and timelines by which you want to achieve those goals. You must also set out a marketing budget and resources (time, workforce etc.). If you do not have the money to hire someone to market the game for you, here are a few things you can do to enhance your total download and sales revenue.

Use social media- Social media is a vibrant marketplace that may have a great positive effect on the total sale and download of your game. If you have many friends on social media, share the game with them first and ask them to share the game with others. This is especially effective if the game is a free version. If your video game has a price tag on it, share the link to the video game with all your friends and ask them to download it. Additionally, social media also has very many developer groups. Join a few of them and contribute to topics. When you have racked up some points, tell the members that you just developed a game and you would love their support. In most cases, programmers are supportive of each other, and you will get some sales.

Use Forums- Forums are also another way to drive up your sales and downloads. They are especially effective because they provide a dedicated user base. For example, if your game is a racing one, you can join a developer's forum that caters to the racing niche. Here, you will find many people willing to download and try your game.

Create a website- This is very critical to your marketing. Most users will often time visit the website of a game they want to buy before they download it. They do this so that they can get more information on the game. Additionally, owning a website dedicated to your game sends a message of professionalism. Additionally, a website gives you more play with keywords and search engine optimization. This can be a gold mine for download and potential sales.

Key point/action step

If you are developing a video game for fun, you can simply publish your game and wait for users to try it. However, if you are doing it for a piece of the $97 billion, you must invest some money into marketing.

Chapter 9: Web industry freelancing and art of domain flipping

With almost all stores and transactions now going online, there is a great demand for people who are able to deal with the more technical aspects to securing their online presence. Web professionals are quite like the carpenters, civil engineers and architects of the online world. And so, if you have a good command of this field and would like to earn extra online, here are a couple of things you can do:

Create tutorials. There are a lot of web enthusiasts who would love to learn how to set up a website, create a good blog design or deal with servers. One can set up a blog and provide quality and targeted tutorials and earn by blog advertising, or readers can also pay a fee for your expertise. Just make sure that people get what they pay for. Earnings can range from $50 to $150.

Design web pages and blogs. The design of a website goes beyond what it 'looks like' but also deals with the interface and ease of navigation. It takes technical knowledge to correctly configure these. You can offer these services to aspiring bloggers or start-up companies.

Selling templates, patterns and icons. If you have a great eye for design and love tinkering with patterns and graphics, you can put up some of your designs for sale. Sites like Theme forest allow you to post your original works, and interested users can buy them directly from the site. This is a great way to produce passive income from your creativity.

Keep in mind, though, that coming up with profitable designs takes years of experience to pull off as it involves an intricate play of shapes, colours and lines.

Finding bugs. In an era of increasing cybercrime, larger companies realize the value of fool-proof software that can prevent hackers from taking advantage of their efforts. Because of this, they offer a hefty amount of cash for people who find vulnerabilities in their codes.

James Forshaw was rewarded $100,000 by Microsoft in 2013 for finding a potential security flaw in one of their software. Bugcrowd is a community of similar people specializing in finding coding glitches. It's pretty much positive reinforcement for people who have incredible skills in order to put their talents to good use instead of resorting to hacking.

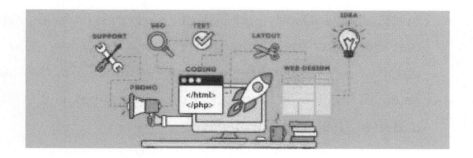

The Art of Domain Flipping

Think of 'domains' as addresses to a house. This refers to the site address of your webpage, like www.ilovethisebook.com, for example. However, to get this address for yourself, you will have to buy it from a web host and domain providers so you could own it. This prevents someone else from the opposite side of the world from putting up a page named www.ilovethisebook.com because that domain name is already yours.

So, what if you have gotten so successful and realized that you would like to rename your site to www.ilovethisebooksomuch.com? You will have to buy this domain again and leave your former webpage address to expire. This will allow the happy lady from the opposite side of the world to finally own a website named www.ilovethisebook.com.

Domain flippers work in between these transactions to make profits. You can go through a list of the unregistered domain in sites like GoDaddy and look out for expired domain names that may be of great value for someone you know. You can purchase www.ilovethisebook.com for about $70, then send an email to a happy lady who would gladly pay you $200 for it. Bravo! The profit is made!

The key in earning through this method is being observant of current trends and insightful for things that may spark interest among people, purchasing domains while their value is still low, then selling it at a great price when you find it most profitable.

It definitely involves risk as you may encounter having to sell domains for zero profit. However, the rewards you get in the process may make this worth a try.

Chapter 10: Some other ideas

Turn Passion to Profit

" What do you really want to do?"

This is one of the most daunting life questions that hit us some time in our teenage years and stretches up until forever. Some people find the answer sooner, and others never really find out. Circumstances often lead us to do things that we'd rather not, and necessity tells us that we cannot always do what we want because the cool things don't always bring food to the table.

What if life finally granted you the opportunity to work on what you've always wanted?

The internet is a world without boundaries. It finds value in the smallest of things, reward your grandest efforts and grants you the possibility of reaching out to all corners of the earth. What may not work in your town may be a hit on a city that is miles away from you. This is a stellar opportunity to finally explore what you've always wanted, feed it to the world wide web and even earn from it! All in the comforts of your home!

Many people have followed their passion and have now gone on to become professional artists, writers, consultants and the like. Do not hesitate to explore your own.

Get Paid for Your Reviews

Do you remember spending a whole day debating with girlfriends on the phone on which makeup was better or what brand of shampoo was the best? Looks like you can actually earn from it!

Again, it all boils down to marketing and advertising. Companies would love to know what you think of their product and are willing to pay you for your opinion.

Vindale Research is an online shopping site that pays you for posting reviews about items that you have bought from their site. You can expect to get paid up to $75 both for answering reviews and surveys on their site. You can make withdrawals via PayPal to ensure the security of your information.

Other websites pay you to review other items like User Testing for website interface reviews ($10 per review), Shvoong for reviews about newspapers, academic papers, books and random articles (payout depends on revenue of the product).

Review Stream is another popular pay-for-review website that pays $2 for every review on hot topics and also gives additional points when people rate up to your review.

There are a great many legitimate sites that offer payment for each review you give their products; now, isn't that a better way to spend all that energy raving or ranting about various consumer products?

Pay-for-review is another targeted approach for earning extra money. It is a great feedback system that the common consumer can use to reach out to retail companies in order to improve the very products we use.

Getting paid for sharing what you think about your latest purchase seems to be a neat idea, yes?

The Era of Mobile Apps

The smartphone and tablet market are now saturated with apps of all shapes and sizes. While smartphone designs and capabilities are all the craze right now, mobile apps are quickly catching up because they allow you to use your phone for several functionalities that the manufacturer wasn't able to include.

There's an app that measures your heart rate, an app that reads your horoscope for the day, an app that gives directions, an app that plays dice and not to mentions the gazillions of games that are available both in Android's Playstore and I phone's Appstore. The most successful of apps are known to be earning thousands of bucks per month out of user purchases, and believe it or not, Candy Crush is actually earning $947,000 every day. Incredible!

What attracts a lot of people is that it is open to everyone with the right number of tools and knowledge. In spite of the saturated market, people still love to create something that others can use or have fun with, quite similar to publishing e-books. And there's always that hope of being the next viral thing and waking up a millionaire the next day. Remember Flappy Bird?

Creating a mobile app entails a complicated web of wireframing, data integration, user-interface development and design, server-side logic and user management, among others. But the bottom line is to create an app that can delight, entertain or be greatly useful for specific applications.

The interface of the app must be designed in an appealing and engaging manner following the modern laws of design and user-friendliness. It has to be comprehensively tested and refined with zero to minimal bugs.

Android will let your apps launch untested in the Playstore, while iPhone requires all apps to undergo a review process that takes about a week. Once it's out there, your apps will be tested through user reviews and purchases.

One thing that developers forget, though, is to advertise their apps. This is essential if you really want to earn.

Bookkeeping

Another technical skill that could be put to use is bookkeeping. This basically entails keeping a clean record of all the cash flow details of a particular company or individual. This includes keeping track of all invoices, receipts, earnings and payables. This is gaining increasing momentum in several countries because more and more entrepreneurs are trying to enter businesses without knowing how to streamline their cash flow. This is critical to businesses because it allows you to keep track of your collectibles and your deadlines. Unmanaged finances will only cost a business more money and a bad reputation in the future.

This type of industry is good for people who don't get bored with numbers, have an eye for detail and the integrity to keep records clean. Various online courses are now being offered for people who would like to get the hang of the industry, but one may require a couple of years of actual training before gaining enough reputation to work as an independent bookkeeper.

Armed with sufficient storage, reliable accounting software, and a great ability to organize, bookkeeping can be a great work-at-home job for people. The average bookkeeper earns $25 to $40 per hour but can also increase depending on workload and location.

Adding tax preparation services can also increase your value as a bookkeeper, and so does an accounting background. Having business cards and referrals from former satisfied clients will also boost your reputation.

Pay-to-Click Sites (PTC)

Clixsense, Probux, Neobux and Fusebux are some of the most trusted online sites when it comes to pay-to-click industries. This is by far the easiest way to earn money on the internet. It basically starts with you clicking the "Register now" button and signing up for their services; then, you start to familiarize yourself with the website interface while earning. It will not require you to pay upon registration though some of them may require an optional 'investment' for you to grow your earnings faster, although you'll do just fine even without availing of this option.

The main mechanism of earning is by clicking and watching 30-second ads and quickly moving on to the next, depending on how much you intend to earn.

Pros: This is the easiest way to earn on the internet; no experience or necessary skill sets are required, and you decide how much time you are willing to allot. They also design the site and advertisements well enough to keep you engaged and entertained during the whole session.

The product also has a community forum where users can share ideas and help in navigating the site, which makes it all the more legitimate because you are confident that other people are really using and getting paid with it.

These companies also make use of PayPal, Payza, Perfect Money, SolidTrust Pay, and Ego Pay, which allow users to receive their payment without really revealing too much financial information.

Cons: In as much as they provide the easiest ways to earn money, they also have the lowest rates of payment. Clixsense has one of the highest payouts, which is $0.02 per click.

These sites also have a minimum payout threshold, meaning you have to accumulate a certain amount before you are able to withdraw to your account. Clixsense has a minimum payout level of $10, which means you'll have to click through the ads 500 times before you are able to withdraw. That's about four and a half hours of viewing ads! As you see, it may take a long while before you are really able to withdraw a substantial amount.

Other sites offer a smaller payout threshold like Neobux that only requires $2, and Probux, for only $5. However, the rate per click is also lower.

Earning PTC ads is a great idea only when you intend for this to be an additional activity while browsing the internet. You'll also need to be extra patient with it because it will take a while before you are able to really earn.

Value in the Smallest Efforts

Companies spend a great bulk of their budget on advertising and will go to great lengths just to extend their brand reach and to understand how their consumers perceive their products. This concept has driven an online industry that allows people to earn dollars by doing very simple tasks like clicking links, answering surveys, viewing advertisements and the like. Many people are flocking to this kind of industry because of the promise of earning with very little effort.

As attractive as it is, this type of industry is also one of the most prone to abuse and scams and must therefore be examined carefully before getting involved. If you feel like the pay is way too large for the equivalent effort required, follow your gut feel and check if it is a scam.

Nevertheless, there are legitimate companies who really use these methods as part of their advertising, and it's a great deal for people who want to earn extra bucks for a couple of minutes. If you can spend a whole hour watching cat videos, then the idea of answering a 15-minute survey for five dollars shouldn't be a bad idea, yes?

No effort is too small for the internet. Everything has value.

Conclusion:

To conclude, business valuation, if done correctly, can work in your favor. That is also true for the intended buyer. Business valuation can be done in-house or through the help of certified public accountants and business valuators.

It is also very important to discuss matters about selling your business with people around you (business partners, workmates and family members) to help you cement the idea. Once a business changes hands, it is permanent until the current owner decides to sell again.

Placing value on your business and eventually selling it off is the culmination of all the years, tears and hard work of building the business and running its day-to-day operations. Some business owners are anxious about separating themselves from their own businesses. In the end, through proper business valuation, you will be able to see your business as it is. It is just an income-generating machine that you built and developed.

Remember that although this book provides you with the basic knowledge on how to place a value on your business' worth, the need for professional business valuators and certified public accountants are still necessary. The practical knowledge that they possess concerning this aspect of the business is one gained through constantly perfecting their craft.

This book aims to open your eyes to what goes behind the scenes during these transactions and help you understand the business valuation process. The simple action steps provided in each chapter and subchapters are there for you to perform on your own business.

Finally, it is imperative that you are keen on the details of your own business and are meticulous about keeping records. These records will help you find the true value of your business.

Lightning Source UK Ltd.
Milton Keynes UK
UKHW020913140321
380286UK00001B/21